I want to be a
SOCCER PLAYER

By Eugene Baker

Illustrated by Ralph Canaday

CHILDRENS PRESS, CHICAGO

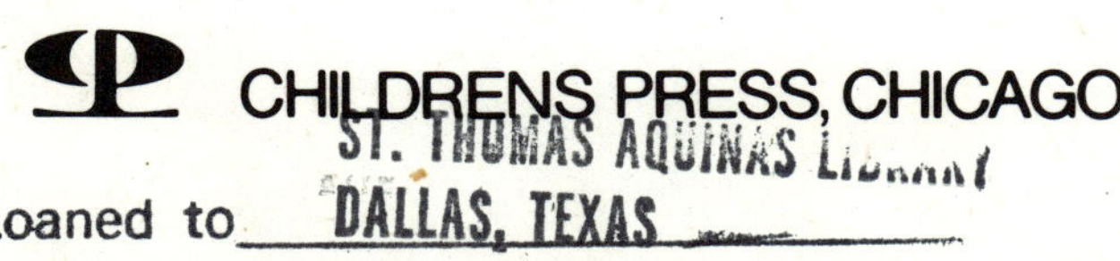

Library of Congress Cataloging in Publication Data

Baker, Eugene H
  I want to be a soccer player.

  1. Soccer—Juvenile literature.   I. Canaday, Ralph.
II. Title.
GV943.25.B34   796.33'42   75-37642
ISBN 0-516-01734-9

SCORE! The crowd roared.

"What a great game," cried Julie.

"Soccer is fast and exciting," said Steve.

Julie, Scott, Steve, John, Nancy, and Jim were members of the Pee-Wee Soccer League at their park. Their team was named the Cardinals.

Going home on the bus, everyone talked about the game.

"Boy, they sure run a lot," said Nancy.

Their coach, Mr. Anderson, smiled. "That's true. Play rarely stopped. I knew you would enjoy seeing the professionals play."

The next morning the team met in the park district fieldhouse. Mr. Anderson came in. He was carrying a chalk board and some diagrams.

"Before we go out onto the field, let's talk about soccer rules and equipment." He took some chalk. "This is what a soccer field looks like. The field may be bigger or smaller."

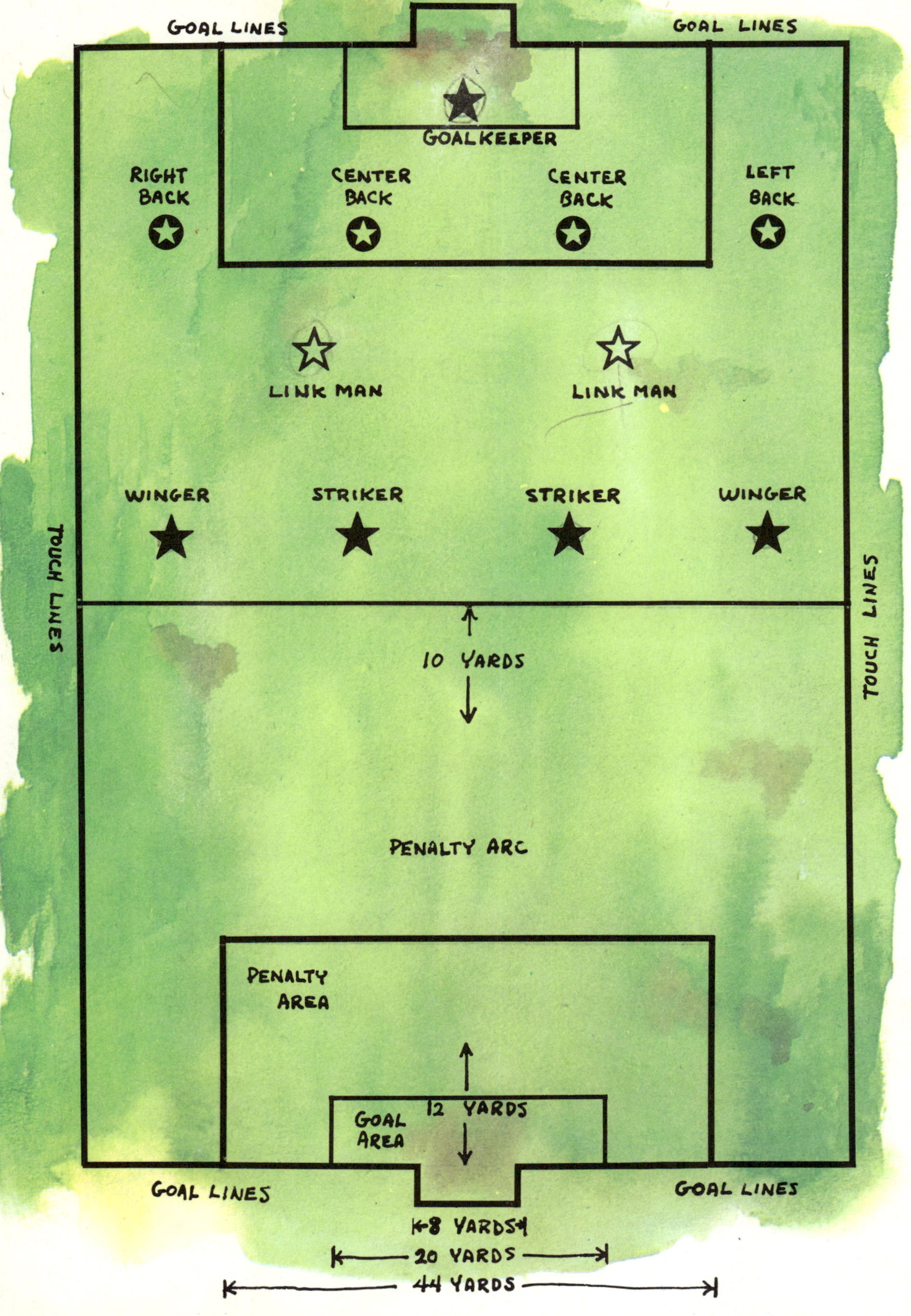

GOAL LINES
GOAL LINES
GOALKEEPER
RIGHT BACK
CENTER BACK
CENTER BACK
LEFT BACK
LINK MAN
LINK MAN
WINGER
STRIKER
STRIKER
WINGER
TOUCH LINES
TOUCH LINES
10 YARDS
PENALTY ARC
PENALTY AREA
GOAL AREA
12 YARDS
GOAL LINES
GOAL LINES
8 YARDS
20 YARDS
44 YARDS

Mr. Anderson made an X in the middle of the diagram. "Players line up to start on their half of the field. To begin play, you must be at least ten yards from the ball."

"If the ball is kicked out of bounds, play stops. A player from the opposing team then must kick or throw the ball into the playing area."

"Please try not to commit fouls," Mr. Anderson added. "Do not kick other players. Do not trip or push anyone. Do not deliberately run into anyone.

17
8
BUY
STOC

We want to have a lot of fun; no one should get hurt."

"If there is a foul, a penalty kick is awarded. Penalty kicks are taken from this spot in front of the goal."

Julie waved her hand, "We saw that last night, Mr. Anderson. Only the kicker and the goalkeeper stood in the penalty area."

"That's right, Julie," said Mr. Anderson. "The object of soccer is to pass the ball between members, then score between the goal posts. Most players kick the ball with their feet or hit it with their heads."

"Where do we stand when the game starts?" asked Scott.

Mr. Anderson picked up a chart. "There are eleven

positions in soccer. Each of you
will try out for the different
positions."

"How did soccer begin?"
asked Nancy.

Mr. Anderson smiled. "In England in the 1800's, the colleges got together and formed the English football clubs."

Scott and Steve looked at each other. Then they said together, "Football?"

"Yes," laughed Mr. Anderson. "In England, soccer is called

football. O.K., Cardinals, that's enough talk. Let's go out onto the field and practice."

Mr. Anderson placed the soccer ball on the ground. "You may kick the ball three ways. You can use your instep or the top of your foot. You can use the outer or inner side of your foot, like this. Or you may use your heel. Most good soccer players kick with their instep. Today, practice passing the ball to your teammates. I want quick

short passes. Use the inside of
your foot."

The team practiced passing
the soccer ball.

"Next, we will practice dribbling the ball. You must move the ball downfield in front of you. Kick it gently with one foot, then the other. Be sure and keep the ball close to your feet."

A few days later, Mr. Anderson explained a new skill. "This is called heading." Coach

Anderson hit the ball downfield
with his head. "Sometimes you
can score a goal by heading the
ball. Please notice I use my
forehead."

After many days of practice, the park district games began. The Cardinals did well. Julie and Nancy were excellent at passing and dribbling the ball. Scott and Steve were stars on defense. They were also good at tackling. They could kick the ball away from an opponent with their feet.

By the end of the summer the
Cardinals had made it into the
play-offs. In the quarter-finals,
they beat the Pirates. The score
was four to two.

The next game was played in the rain. They beat the Bisons one to nothing. Steve had scored the only goal on a penalty shot.

Mr. Anderson was happy. "Next Saturday we play for the championship."

Saturday was warm and sunny. The Cardinals warmed up on the field slowly. Julie looked over to Nancy. "You know, the Knights have only lost one game all summer."

"I know," Nancy nodded. "Their goalkeeper sure is fast."

The team gathered around Mr. Anderson. "Well, this is it. Play hard. Remember your passing. Watch for an open person. Do your best."

The game was tied. With two minutes left to play, the score

was Cardinals two and Knights two.

Suddenly, Scott tackled the ball away from an opponent. The ball shot straight up in the air. Scott sent a long head pass

down the field. Steve went
racing downfield to catch it.
Julie, her red ponytail flying,
was right behind him. Steve
dribbled past several defensive
players and headed toward the
goal.

Just inside the goal area, he headed to his left. Julie cut to the right. The goalkeeper raced toward Steve. Just then, Steve sent a quick pass to Julie on his right. Julie kicked. The ball shot into the right corner of the goal net. The goalkeeper fell to the ground, just missing the ball.

The crowd, coaches, and
parents cheered, "Hurray,
Cardinals." The game was over.

The final score was the Cardinals three and the Knights two.

"Nice shot, Julie," yelled Mr. Anderson.

Julie waved her hand, "We worked together as a team. You know, coach," Julie said with a twinkle in her eye, "some day I want to be a professional soccer player."

Mr. Anderson laughed,
"That's fine with me. O.K.,
Cardinals, I'm buying ice cream
for everyone."

About the Author:

Dr. Baker was graduated from Carthage College, Carthage, Illinois. He got his master's degree and doctorate in education at Northwestern University. He has worked as a teacher, as a principal, and as a director of curriculum and instruction. Now he works full time as a curriculum consultant. His practical help to schools where new programs are evolving is sparked with his boundless enthusiasm. He likes to see social studies and language arts taught with countless resources and many books to encourage students to think independently, creatively, and critically. The Bakers, who live in Arlington Heights, Illinois, have a son and two daughters.

About the Artist:

Ralph Canaday has been involved in all aspects of commercial art since graduation from the Art Institute of Chicago in 1959. As an illustrator, designer and sculptor his work has appeared in many national publications, textbooks, and corporate promotional material. He is currently working on his "Famous Aviators" series, a collection of life-size bronze busts in limited edition of such aviators as the Baron Von Richthofen, Charles Lindbergh, Eddie Rickenbacker and Amelia Earhart. His knowledge of aviation history garnered through years of collecting, reading and flying have made him an "expert" in this area. He is also continually working on his aviation illustrations which are a natural adjunct to his "hobby." Ralph lives in Hanover Park, Illinois with his wife Arlene, who is also in publishing.